I ANGELS DON'T HAVE WINGS

The

Master Teacher

Connection

DR. ERIKA J. CHOPICH
Co-Creator of *INNER BONDING*

Published 2025 by Gildan Media LLC
aka G&D Media
www.GandDmedia.com

FIRST EDITION: 2025

Front cover design by Tom McKeveny

Interior design by Meghan Day Healey of Story Horse, LLC.

Library of Congress Cataloging-in-Publication Data is available upon
request

ISBN: 978-1-7225-0713-8

10 9 8 7 6 5 4 3 2 1

Contents

Part Three
Making Contact 57

Part Four
The Teachings 75

Introduction

"On the most sleepless night of 1992 I resentfully sat up and turned on the light. I began searching for the origin of the torment that shattered my sleep that night. Even in the fog of restlessness, as a clinical psychotherapist I knew that the voices keeping me awake were not from any psychopathology—I just did not fit any diagnostic criteria. I was recovering well from my bout with Epstein-Bar virus so I was sure the cause was not physical. As a minister, I had never experienced a Divine vision so I did not attribute this event to that. The voices however echoed in my head until I couldn't sleep. They were the voices of strangers in the night, and even more upsetting, was the experience of the voices coming from far across my normally cozy bedroom. I decided the best thing was to ignore it, since I couldn't stop it anyway. It was probably better to deal with this further in the clarity and safety of tomorrow's light. I patted my golden retriever, Mandy, on the head and determined to surrender to sleep, I flopped back into my pillow.

My body suddenly snapped rigid with the terror of recollection as I was jerked backward into a very early childhood memory. I recalled the feelings of my toddler's body as I sat in the grass behind our little house in Pennsylvania. I could feel the rhythm as I rocked gently back and forth on the green lawn. I looked upward and there they were, matted by the blue sky! My friends! I remembered the nameless faces and friendly voices I had encountered so many times as I child. I could see them and hear them, and they always felt good. The faces were smiling and fun and they spoke in loving, cooing tones. Why didn't anyone else ever talk about them? Were they a secret? Looking back I felt grateful that as a child I never shared this experience with anyone. I might have been forced to spend my development in the treatment of juvenile schizophrenia!

In the reality of that long night though, I didn't feel comfort or friendship, only anguish. "They're back" I thought and all I wanted to do was hide. "Who *are* these people? Why don't they leave me alone?" I thought I had outgrown this junk! My head swirled with questions, anger, anxiety and those damn voices!

In frustration I begged out loud, "Who are you?" Instead of an immediate answer my eyes started to catch a glimmer or shadow in front of me. I stared a little longer as curiosity overtook my fear and slowly the glimmer of light began to take form, a person's form! Was there a homeless person in my house? "Who are you?" I repeated from a softer place within me. The age-graveled voice responded, "Daughter, I am your Teacher." In a dazed and confused state I knew that I had had enough so I immediately and promptly fell asleep.

In the days that followed I discussed and explored my continuing experiences with my friend in Los Angeles, Margaret Paul. I tried to find an acceptable and comfortable explanation for these events. Perhaps it was from the virus I had, or maybe living in Santa Fe's seven thousand foot altitude was affecting me. Margaret however reminded me of what I taught in workshops so often, that it is always better to face your fear then to run. So I decided to put aside my judgment of what was happening to me and adopt an openness to learning. I would meet with this form that speaks that very night.

That evening I sat on my bed and with surprising ease summoned "the thing." Respectfully though timidly I spoke in a hushed tone that I could easily deny. "Are you still here?" Oh God, did that feel stupid! "Hello daughter" the voice spoke with caring, and as it did, I saw the form grow into detail. I saw before me and about three feet away, an elderly woman in her seventies or so, with gray hair, faded brown eyes and the kind of face people always photograph in black and white. She seemed to be about five feet tall but I wasn't sure because she was slightly bent with age. I rubbed my eyes, but she was still there! "Hello" I fumbled, "Who are you?" I saw empathy in her eyes for my great confusion, "I am your Master Teacher." she said softly. I wanted to throw-up. This was too weird for me . . . I don't like airy-fairy stuff . . . I'm done . . . Don't talk to me anymore, my head was throbbing and I didn't like this.

That was my first adult experience with a Master Teacher. In the weeks that followed I continued "talking" to my new friend while discussing the experiences with Margaret. We explored many avenues in seeking the answers to our questions. Who were these Teachers? Why can I see them? Does everyone have one? What is the purpose of this ability? Is there anything dark or sinister about this Teacher? Is this experience from any physical or emotional syndrome? Could we actually trust the information that was being imparted to me? It all seemed more like fun until the day came when my Teacher told me that I could see the Master Teacher of any other person! "That's it!" I thought. "I do not want this anymore. That is too weird for me and I know what you will expect of me. NO!!" The harder I tried to smother the voice of my Teacher the clearer it became! I pleaded with God in desperation, "Please God. Give this to some New Ager who *wants* it!"

My resistance was deeply grounded. I had had a life of service to others in my ministry, medicine, and psychology. The very foundation of all of my training was in science and service to God, and I, as a very logical, rational, and respected clergy/psychologist and author, would not entertain or pursue any parapsychological bunk! Sometimes though, God has a different plan for us, and I eventually had to surrender my resistance in order to gain my peace. Surrender has always been hard for me. I understood the concept of spiritual surrender and had, as a minister, been devoted to that process. This, however, was surrendering to something that I didn't understand, couldn't explain, and wasn't sure I should trust. For me the path to accepting the Teachers and my ability was twisted and bumpy, difficult, and rewarding, confrontive and peaceful all at the same time. Before long, however, I was "reading" for other people. With the help of my Teacher I can see and hear the individual Teacher that each person has.

It has taken me a very long time to gain comfort in my ability and to integrate these experiences into my spiritual belief system. I have an ability, but one that other people can develop too. I am not a channeler or psychic nor am I a medium or seer. I use no trance states. I am very sure I am not an enlightened master or guru. I am still the same person I always was, but with an extraordinary amount of information to share. In the following pages you will read about many of the things I have learned about the Master Teachers, some of the experiences I have had in the reading sessions, and what I have been taught by the Teachers. This is a true story. I have taken great care to embellish and exaggerate nothing. You will come to learn as I have, that connecting to our Master Teacher is as natural as breathing. The access to the Teacher is natural, but we have either forgotten how, or were taught not to hear. I retained the ability to hear and so can you.

Part One

THE TEACHERS

Who The Teachers Are

My knowledge of the Master Teachers comes not only from my own relationship with my Teacher, but from the information I have gathered during readings for other people. It has been a wonderful and exciting process to speak with so many of the Teachers.

We all have many spirit guides and helpers around us. Sometimes those guides are relatives who have passed over, or others we do not know but are there to help guide us on our path of highest good. Each of us however, has one Master Teacher who works with us and only us and oversees the guidance we are given.

As with all guides, the Master Teachers once walked this planet and lived as we do. When I see or meet a Teacher I will see a unique body, face, expression, and personality. They choose this form for my benefit and for the benefit of the person for whom I am reading. I believe that if I were to see the Teacher in his or her true form, I would probably see an energy field or spot of light. The Teacher assumes and conveys to me an image of a person. Sometimes they choose how they looked in their last incarnation or they choose an image that is significant to the student. It is much easier to develop feelings for, and connect to, another person than an energy field. I have learned that the personality is not lost in spirit. Some Teachers are unassuming while others are more stoic or animated. The Teachers are as varied in personality as we are.

Through their own growth and evolution they have raised themselves to a level of Master and it is through their work with us that they continue to evolve and grow and move closer to God. I experience the Master Teachers as having endless patience and unconditional love. During a reading I sometimes feel my own frustration mounting as the person resists the truth their Teacher offers, and then I look into the face of their Teacher, and I see the devotion and understanding, love and acceptance that can only come from someone very evolved and very connected to God. As a result, I feel relaxed again as I follow the acceptance and love of the Teacher. For example, a woman for whom I was reading was very intent on getting information about her career. She wanted to know if she should stay in her present job or not, should she keep doing the same work, and when will she make good money. She believed that the answers to these questions would change her life into something wonderful and peaceful. Her Teacher consistently responded with different information. He continually encouraged her to look at her own anger and then proceeded to outline the steps she needed to take to find her peace. He clearly illustrated to her that her answers were not in the material world, but in resolving her angry way of being. Each time the Teacher would respond, she would ask another question about work. I started to feel an incredible frustration that this Master was handing her an obvious life path and she was stuck asking about her boss! In response to my growing frustration the Teacher smiled at me and said, "I am planting seeds. I have faith in her. She will understand this in a day or two. Even as we speak, she knows that her career is not the issue, she is just a little anxious about looking inward." While these words were spoken to me I detected no judgment towards me or the woman, no arrogance, no superiority. There was unconditional love and faith for the person in whom he cared so deeply. In moments my frustration was gone and I was eager to follow the role-modeling of this Master. It was my own judgment and impatience that caused me to feel frustrated and I never forgot this lesson.

When we transition from this planet, many of us will get to be "helpers" of some kind, but to evolve to the level of a Master Teacher (which we all eventually will) will take much work and growth on our parts.

One of the most commonly asked questions during a reading is, "How did my Teacher choose to work with me?" I have always found the answer to this question fascinating. During a person's birth process, the light, or essence of who they are, is very bright. That light seems to call to the Teacher and they feel within their essence, a matching or paring taking place. I have often heard them explain, "I just knew that you were the one I would be working with." It has always been interesting for me to observe the similarities between the Teacher and the person for whom I am reading. There will always be some commonality. The Teachers retain the knowledge and personality of their time spent here, so sometimes I will see a similarity in knowledge areas such as science, or music, or art. Sometimes, I will see similarities on the personality level such as speech patterns or quickness of smile, or sense of humor. Always though, the Teacher and the person look and feel like a perfect match.

There are as many different Teachers as there are people. They seem to have individual areas of expertise as well. Some Teachers are well versed in the areas of physical manifestation on the planet and help their student to build things, earn money, and so on. Other Teachers specialize in creativity or spirituality or carry a strong mother or father energy. It seems that what they have experienced and were interested in on this planet carries over into that life and that acquired knowledge helps guide them to their student. What lessons you are needing in this life and the areas in which you will need help, all become part of the matching process when you are born.

In some cases, a person's life path will take them beyond their Teacher's specialty, in which case they will be given the assistance of a second Teacher. I have found this to be rather rare. Sometimes, the second Teacher is a replacement and sometimes an additional Teacher. Most people seem to retain the same Teacher throughout their lives unless their life has had many traumatic transitions.

The Teacher's Goal

Why we have a Master Teacher seems to be a gift from something higher. Your Teacher has two goals: a goal for his or her own growth and a goal for your growth. It is very clear that your needs for your growth always takes precedence over the Teacher's growth.

Your Teacher grows and evolves by loving you unconditionally and without judgment. You are the center of your Teacher's universe and every thought and action taken by your Teacher has one purpose: to keep you on the path of your highest good. With each passing day your Teacher, through his or her work with you, evolves also until one day they evolve to a state of pure light.

Eileen reflects on her experience with her Teacher:

"After my reading I experienced a feeling that I'd never internalized before. Support, deep love, rest and connection to a divine entity for my own best interest, to myself.

As an incest survivor, I've never before felt that anything divine loves me. There are many things my Teacher will be present for. I am more receptive because my Teacher is devoted to me. I wasn't judged, I was loved. I don't owe him, it is divine love."

Susan experienced healing from her Teacher:

"During the beginning of our relationship I was working on father issues. It was during one of my 'connecting baths' that I was asking for help and I started feeling very connected with a deep warmth emanating from within. I heard this voice say 'I am the father that you have always wanted.' I then felt this incredibly beautiful feeling of total love encompass me. Tears gently flowed down my cheeks and the little girl inside of me felt as if she would never be totally alone again."

The Teachers are here to guide and nudge us onto our most spiritual path of highest good. Often your Teacher will devise events to encourage your lessons and guide your paths. Have you ever had the awareness that so many relationships or events in your life are repeated over and over? That is most likely the influence of your Teacher helping you to see the patterns in the choices you make.

We can assist our Teachers by developing direct contact with them. That is, learning awareness of their presence and developing the ability to communicate with them directly. This process is natural and easy and I have come to believe that we were always meant to "hear" our Teachers but we either forgot how, or were taught not to listen. When we have no awareness of our Teachers they assist us through others means. They will guide us by directing life events for us to experience or by having us cross paths with certain people. They are constant and always there helping even if we don't know it. If, on the other hand, we have direct access and communication with our Teacher, the process of guiding us changes dramatically. They are able to answer questions and teach and suggest and as a result the whole process moves more quickly. This is as exciting to the Teachers as it is to us. Be assured however, that a Teacher will never tell you *what* to do. That would be controlling instead of Teaching. They never want to interfere with our journey or decide our path. They wish only to assist us on the paths *we choose for ourselves.* We will explore further the process of contacting your Teacher later on.

Power Animals

n addition to our Teachers and guides we also have with us one or more animals to assist us. I use the term *power animal* borrowed from the Native Americans because it is the best concept I have found for explaining their presence. The power animals are like spiritual pets. They are loyal and protective and work to help us with the day to day business of living on the planet. Your animal tries to keep you out of harm's way and lets you know when you are in a situation that is not safe for you. These animals are very loving and rarely leave your side. They are playful and affectionate and love finding ways to help you. Very often I will ask my animals to remind me to call so-and-so or to help me with a project or even to help me find a parking place!

The animals also help us in another way. They bring to us a specific energy and lesson that we are needing in this lifetime. For example the eagle, which brings to us the ability to connect to the divine, is very different from the mountain lion which teaches leadership. As people experience different transitions and changes in their lives, they may acquire different animals to help them. During readings I have encountered people who have one animal and people who have many.

I personally have grown accustomed to asking my animals for help in specific ways. They let me know when the mail has arrived, remind me to take my vitamins and alert me to when I am being tricked. Your animal loves to serve you and can do even more for you when you learn to communicate directly with them. We really can "talk to the animals" and even better, they can talk back!

Religion and the Master Teachers

have found that on occasion anxiety about betraying religion, or its dogma, hinders a person from establishing a relationship with their Teacher. While I respect that person's beliefs, I also have found that in many religions there are beliefs that could be interpreted as supporting the concept of spiritual guides such as the Teachers. The exception to this may be Buddhism, although I have done readings for many Buddhists.

Looking at the personal rather than transpersonal concept of God in Hinduism (Saguna Brahman) we think of the nineteenth century saint Ramakrishna and his teaching that "All doctrines are only so many paths; but a path by no means is God Himself. Indeed, one can reach God if one follows any of the paths with whole-hearted devotion." In further teachings he confirms the corporal appearance and visions of Shiva as a teacher.

Hindus believe that the soul (jivas) is spirit rather than body, and that the spirit is not dependent on the body. "Worn-out garments are shed by the body/Worn-out bodies are shed by the dweller." (Bhagavad-Gita). This soul is compelled through each incarnation to ascend through each lifetime until reaching complete identification with God. The four paths to that goal are: through knowledge (jnana), through love (bhakti), through work (karma) and through psychophysical exercises (raja). Of these four trainings (yoga) it is raja, by means of its personal, introverted, psychophysical experiments that visions and apparitions often invade the sought-after experience of the "beyond within." It is very possible that in the altered state achieved by such profound meditative practices, the practitioner spontaneously, if not accidentally, interacts with his/her Teacher (spirit).

By the second century A.D., Taoists had built their religion on rituals and their magical properties. Some of these rituals involved the invoking or sometimes dispelling of ghosts (spirit). The concept was that life-giving force (chi) could be made available to the people through the Taoist priest. Often these healing rituals included encounters with visions, animals and spirits that helped to bring the chi to the person in need.

In the sixth century an angel appeared to Muhammad telling him to "Proclaim in the name of your Lord who created man from blood coagulated! Proclaim: your Lord is wondrous kind, Who teaches by the pen, Things men knew not, being blind" (Koran 96:1-3) The voice of the angel returned repeatedly until Muhammad's life was forever changed. The Koran further teaches that the soul (spirit) upon death enters into heaven or hell where angels are as well.

In Judaism, the Torah refers to angels many times in the five books of Moses. However it is the Kabbalah (the study of Jewish mysticism) that approximates even more closely the concept of the Master Teachers. At the moment of devekuth (cleaving to God) a Kabbalist is said to experience his or her supernatural guide (the maggid).

In the New Testament I have counted one hundred ten references to angels, and in the Old Testament one hundred fifteen. The Bible state in 1 Corinthians 12:7: "But the manifestation of the Spirit is given to every man to profit withal. For to one is given by the Spirit the word of wisdom; to another the word of knowledge by the same Spirit; to another faith by the same Spirit; to another the gifts of healing by the same Spirit; to another the working of miracles; to another prophecy; to another discerning of spirits; to another divers kinds of tongues; to another interpretation of tongues." It is clear to me that the three major branches of Christianity—Roman Catholicism, Eastern Orthodoxy and Protestantism, all maintain a profound belief in spirits and angels.

Catholics do not necessarily expect supernatural experiences in this life. They may, through devout prayer and faith receive some state of grace. While they regularly celebrate prayers, hymns, and feasts to the angels, the Church cautiously regards reported visions and the miracles associated with them. The Catholic Church cannot state unequivocally that these events cannot occur, but may permit the belief of the individual parishioner.

Orthodoxy has a foundational belief in mysticism. All Orthodox are encouraged through an ascetical life to discover the mystical life. One of the charisms, and a minor one to be sure, is the gift of visions. The Feast of the Archangels is celebrated in November and prayer are invoked not only to the angels, but also to one's particular guardian angel. A hymn is sung that the angels ". . . fence us around with their intercessions and shelter us under their protecting wings of immortal glory." In the Philokalia (a collection of texts written by spiritual masters of the Orthodox Church) St. Theodoros states, "Being servants of love and peace the angels. . . . try to develop spiritual contemplation within us in the achieving of every form of blessing."

Protestantism holds at its center the Bible, believing that it is literally "God's Word." With this doctrine one would assume that a belief in the angels and the Holy Spirit is essential, and it is to some degree. While vital life experiences are often believed to be the work of the Holy Spirit, a direct manifestation of spirit may also be regarded as evil. There are many, many denominations within the Protestant branch. Perhaps the one that would regard the Teachers as suspicious would be those of the fundamental Christian religions. In 2 Corinthians 11:14 Paul states; ". . . Satan himself transforms himself into an angel of light." To this I can only respond that the angels were created by God (Col. 1:16) to have charge over us (Ps 91:11), to guide us (Gen 24:40), to provide for us (1 Kings 19:5–8), to protect us (Psalm 34:7), direct us (Acts 8:26), comfort us (Acts 27:23,24) and to minister to us (Heb. 1:14).

Part Two

THE READINGS

How I Read

have done readings for hundreds of people who wished to meet their Teachers. Occasionally, I read for children or infants as well. Parents often wanted to know more about their child's path, abilities and health. They were often guided in better parenting techniques as well. Generally, though, I read mostly for adults. I asked only for the person's name and wanted to know nothing else about them. I did not need to know their backgrounds, problems, or questions. Their Teacher already knew what they needed and my knowing anything about the person could have resulted in projecting my own biases. I usually started a reading by choosing an incense or fragrance I liked and dispersed it around the outside of the person's body. My favorite was sage and in taking the time to do this, several things would happen.

First of all, I was clearing the person's auric field of any negative or stressful energy and this felt good to them, while making the reading easier. As I did this, I was able to watch the person's energy flow through the meridians and chakras in their body. A person's life energy or *Chi* appears very sparkling and flows in definite directions along the neural pathways of the body. The important aspect of this is that I can see where their energy is blocked. When a blockage occurs the energy will either stop at the blockage or in some cases flow around the blockage and continue on. Sometimes I saw the block on the physical level and sometimes I saw it on an emotional level. Usually, I had no idea why the person was blocked, but their Teacher knew and would explain what it was and what could be done about it. Teachers always seemed concerned about the balance of energy in our bodies. In fact, they probably care for our "temples" better than we do! At first I had difficulty reconciling this information with my training in western medicine. I had been certified as a paramedic, a lab assistant, a dental assistant, and a surgical technician. I was open to ideas about acupuncture, and my studies in religion had familiarized me with the Hindu concepts of chakras and the Tao concept of Chi, but healing and understanding energies was difficult for me. For example I commonly saw food allergies in the person for whom I was reading. Traditionally, a food allergy is an auto-immune response to something we are sensitive to. In mild forms the allergy can produce rashes or hives but in extreme cases may cause an anaphylactic response, that is, respiratory failure and shock. In terms of energy however, the food to which one is sensitive can cause an energy block that alters or stops the flow of Chi to an organ and thereby affects the balance of energy throughout the body. Many times we have an allergy to something that blocks our energy and we don't even know it because the energy block is nearly imperceptible. The result, however, can be a chronic persistent problem to one organ or more. I came to know that our health is very important to our Teachers.

Elaine describes her experience of this part of the reading:

"Having my food allergies shown has been amazingly helpful. For several years prior to our meeting, I'd been having lung problems—breathing problems actually. My doctor had taken at least three sets of lung x-rays during a six or seven year period because of my complaints. My problems were not obvious, but sometimes getting deep breaths was impossible, and it felt as though I still smoked, even though I'd stopped ten years before. When the lungs would act up, I felt very tired as well. My lungs were always clear and my doctor never found anything wrong.

"At our first meeting Erika told me she saw the discomfort in my lungs and my fatigue. Immediately she said it was caused by allergies—dairy and wheat. The adrenals were being affected and causing me to be very tired.

"For the next two weeks I didn't eat the offending foods—then I decided to 'test' either her or my Teacher, Richard. I had pizza and milk. Within hours I felt the effects on my energy levels, and by the next morning I was having difficulty breathing and I was exhausted. Oh well; I do miss the foods; I have to admit that."

Peggy had a similar experience:

"The most important revelation my Master Teacher gave me was that I had a severe allergy to refined sugar, milk, and wheat products. I never thought I could give it all up, especially the sugar. I thought I would try to over the weekend. Amazingly it went so well, I never went back. My stomach pains I have suffered from for many years are completely gone. I do not have food cravings anymore."

After smudging with sage and looking at the person's body, I'd close my eyes in order to contact my Teacher and asked her to introduce me to the subject's Master Teacher. Almost immediately I could see the person's power animal and then a "person." After establishing that the person is, in fact, the subject's Master Teacher, I ask the Teacher if they have a name or how they would like to be addressed. Often, they offer a name and, in some cases, they will choose something like Grandfather. After welcoming the Teacher I allowed them to direct the session from that point on. They knew what their "student's" questions were and knew what information to pass to the person through me. The entire content of the session was up to the discretion of the Teacher. Sometimes if there was information they didn't want me to know I could sense a "veiling" that took place. There was a definite curtain that droped at some point, often about the outcome of something. I would become very aware of an area the Teacher did not wish to discuss.

From that point on we engaged in conversation, answered questions, and received guidance. Since I used no trance states with myself or them, the person was free to ask questions, take notes, or whatever they needed. The reading was not fragile or easily disturbed and looked quite normal and animated.

Frequency

n his book *Hyperspace* (Oxford University Press 1994), author Michio Kaku, a professor in theoretical physics states: "Simply put, the matter in the universe and the forces that hold it together, which appear in a bewildering, infinite variety of complex forms, may be nothing but different vibrations of hyperspace." All matter vibrates at a specific frequency. The book you are reading, your body, the furniture around you, all subtly vibrate from the movement of the electrons in the molecules. This vibration has a frequency; therefore, all matter resonates at various frequencies. People are different than objects because our frequency raises and lowers throughout the day in a rhythmic pattern. The function of the pineal gland in the brain is to regulate our frequency and rhythm, and this is done as an involuntary function for the most part. I was able to perform the readings because I have voluntary control over my pineal gland and can raise my frequency at will. When my frequency is high, I can contact my Teacher, when it goes even higher, I can see someone else's Teacher. I often compare this to blood pressure. We don't normally think much about it as it rises and falls throughout the day. We can however, if we need to, learn to control our blood pressure through biofeedback and meditation techniques. Although I was born with the ability to alter my frequency at will, it can also be learned and developed.

The first step in learning to contact your Teacher and animals is to learn to raise your frequency. This is not difficult, nor is it mystical and you don't need to be enlightened! It just takes a little practice as you will see later on.

The Connections

Readings were generally easy and flowing for me. There were, however, exceptions. If the person I was reading for had a personality that was more closed than open, I would have to exert a great deal of effort in order to hear what their Teacher was saying. It is similar to listening to a talk radio show and the person's closed energy is the static. The more closed they were the more static I heard. Angry personalities were even more difficult. Since during a reading my frequency is very high, I was in a very vulnerable and open state. Another person's anger at that moment felt sharp and actually caused pain in my head and torso.

You may be wondering why a person would be angry or closed during a reading. First of all it is important to remember that people have very compelling reasons for the way they feel and act. Issues from the past and learned beliefs influence our way of being and our personality. As a result, some people are easy-going, relaxed, and open while others may be anxious and angry as a way of being in the world. It may not be the reading that caused their anger; it may be how they operate in their lives.

Secondly, the very idea of the Master Teacher is, for some, a difficult belief as it was for me. So difficult in fact that sometimes the very heart of the matter is a faith issue. Imagine that for most of your life you had been taught one doctrine, say Christianity or Buddhism or whatever. You have lived your life by that doctrine and yet feel as though something is missing. You need more peace or joy or love and no matter what you try, the good feelings escape you. So you practice your doctrine and faith even harder in the hope that a more disciplined spirituality will bring you that for which you have so long yearned. Finally, you find yourself sitting in my office at the urging of a friend who tells you about a Teacher who will help you. In a heartbeat you are being smoked with sage and watching a crazy lady talk to someone you can't see! Then the conflict really begins. You think, "If there really is a Teacher in this room or this lady knows too much about me, it will go against everything I have learned!" Sometimes the pressure of that situation is very difficult for the person in front of me and the anger and mistrust they display is understandable, yet difficult for both of us. I have always believed however, that the person in front of me believes to some degree and is at least partially open or they would not have come to see me.

I have noticed during readings that some people are offered proof of their Teacher's existence and others are not. By proof I mean that the Teacher will give me detailed information to convey that I could not possibly know. Information like names of spouses, friends, life events, losses or illnesses, travels to specific places, recent changes in daily routine, name changes. It was entirely up to the Teacher what information I would be given, and they seemed to choose that based on what their "student" was needing. Whether a reading was very detailed in information or more general in nature was outlined by the Teacher and always it seemed to be exactly right for that person.

I recall reading for a young man, James, who had a very open nature. He had no expectations about the reading and was open for any helpful information that he might gain. During the reading his Teacher said "I think it would be helpful to your process if you would use your Tibetan Meditation bowl more." As I repeated the words, I saw the shock in his face and I wondered what was happening (I wasn't even sure what a Tibetan Meditation bowl was!). James told me it was something he had purchased just a few weeks prior to our session and that he was using it in his meditations less and less. After that his Teacher continued to provide me with very detailed and specific information. By the end of the session I could see the peace on James's face as he realized that he truly was not alone on his path, and his love and belief in his Teacher was growing.

You might think that these moments of extreme detail are something to which I had grown accustomed. I can assure that I have not and I don't think it will ever feel commonplace to me. I still felt startled and delighted each and every time for I know that the details cannot come from me.

Not everyone had the same profound experience during a reading. Some people insisted on getting answers to "fortune-telling" type questions. They would ask, "How can I get more money? Is my boyfriend *the* relationship? Should I change jobs?" Very often the answer to these kinds of questions was. . . . silence. The Teacher said nothing to me and that was what I told them. If at this point the person became angry and demanding, I sometimes felt like stopping the reading, but their Teacher would often have a different idea about things so I continued.

One woman, Jean, had become frustrated with me during the reading because her Teacher would not tell her how to get her boyfriend to pay more attention to her. Just as I had begun to feel bogged-down, her Teacher smiled lovingly and said, "Jean, it takes more energy to complain than to accept, that is why you are always tired." It was like watching an ice cube in a four hundred degree oven. Jean's anger melted and her heart opened, "How did you know I was tired every day?" she asked. "I didn't," I said, "but your Teacher knows everything about you." In a few well-chosen and well-timed words, Jean's Master Teacher had addressed her neediness, her fatigue, and her faith issues all while helping her to open! In the ten years I did family therapy I had never done that with one sentence, and nothing I can do as a minister has been more restoring to a person's faith! I was profoundly struck by the Godly love and acceptance of this Teacher. I felt happy and excited for Jean and peacefully connected to God at that moment myself. Whenever I am witness to Divine mystery I am humbled by the experience.

Jean's experience was a good example of a Teacher communicating in words. This is not always the case. Teachers will often communicate with pictures, thoughts, feelings, ideas, and concepts. I have experienced many Teachers using combinations of things to communicate something to me. There really is no "cosmic voice" coming from outside yourself; it is just information being exchanged on any level that you or I can receive it. Your Teacher will know what you are most sensitive to and will communicate with you on that level, or use a combination of things.

I recently had an experience that illustrates this point further. I was going shopping with Margaret. In the car I told her that I had had a song going around and around in my head since awakening that morning. She asked what was the song and I told her," It's from the Wizard of Oz, you know that part where they finally find the Emerald city and the Munchkins sing: 'You're out of the woods, You're out of the dark, step into the light.' Don't you think that's strange since I haven't seen that movie in a long while?" Margaret smiled and said, "Erika, don't you think that could be your Teacher?" With that awareness and my openness to the message, the song stopped. My receiver had been turned on, but I hadn't been getting the message. Thankfully, our Teachers are persistent enough and clever enough to deliver the message even when we are "off."

The Number One Question

The most commonly asked question during a reading is: "What is my purpose in life?" I always eagerly awaited the answer too, and there are as many answers to that question as there are Teachers. The answer a Teacher gave depended entirely on what the person I was reading for needed. Teachers would address that question in one of two ways: spiritually or on the physical, earthly, level.

Spiritually, a Teacher would direct the person to examine the lessons they are receiving in life. For example the Teacher might say, "Your main purpose is to heal your neediness in this life and everything around you is a tool for doing just that." There was often an attempt to nudge the person from a material, physical, goal-oriented way of living on the planet into an inward journey of growth and connection to something greater.

Jean shares the experience of her reading:

"Through the help of Erika Chopich, I had my first encounter with my Master Teacher, and since then, approximately eight months ago, my life has significantly changed. I have gone from a state of desperation, that is, crying in the night, and experiencing a terrible and overwhelming feeling of aloneness to a state of spiritual enlightenment which I can best describe as an intense awareness that spirits or Master Teachers really do exist to guide us along our spiritual pathway to God. I cannot put into words how much this revelation has lightened this heavy burden that had weighed on my heart and soul for a lifetime. The heaviness of voice that said I was in this life to do everything myself and that I really had nobody to turn to and really had nobody who understood me—not my husband nor my highly critical parents.

"My first encounter with my Teacher was the single most positive and powerful experience of my life. Here is what happened: I walked into the incense scented room and sank down into the sofa. Erika sat across from me and was not what I had pictured her. Instead of old and craggy with glazed over eyes and crystals about her neck, she was youthful with vibrant dancing eyes. I'll never forget her exciting sparkling eyes—in them you could tell she had lived a long time even though she was so young.

Erika soon raised her vibrational frequency and brought my Teacher into the room. I remember feeling a warm tingling strong vibration throughout my body. I am not a psychic nor am I a person with any mental disability. I am, however, open-minded and sensitive and what I felt that day I now realize was the energy of my Master Teacher. The vibrational sensation lasted for several seconds. It is hard to describe with mere words the intense love and reassurance I felt being communicated to me. It was such an intense spiritual experience that I wept. I had been feeling so desperately alone only moments before. Erika spoke to my Master Teacher who proceeded to tell her that I needed spiritual healing before I would ever really know myself and my purpose here on earth. I think this is the case with so many of us and I can only say that having discovered my Master Teacher has put meaning into my life and given me a spiritual pathway to follow."

Jean was lovingly nudged by her Teacher from an earthly to a spiritual focus of awareness. This was the direct result of her Teacher's guidance and not from anything I did or said personally. As a matter of fact, I was as intrigued by her Teacher's wisdom as Jean was!

Sometimes these experiences happened long distance, without my being in the room. I did a reading for Vivian on the telephone who had a similar experience:

"I met Erika about a year ago and my life has not been the same since. Our first introduction or session was via the telephone, and I must admit I was a bit suspicious of its success. Within minutes though I knew that I was speaking not only to Erika but also to my Master Teacher. As I listened attentively, I felt my body responding to the truth, I felt the tell-tale signs: the chills up and down my spine, the warm tingling of my legs and my feet, the opening of my heart, soft and responsive. But more than that I felt the presence of my Teacher like never before.

Words cannot fully describe this experience. The fact is that for once in my life I did not feel alone, I did not feel that aching emptiness I was so used to. An amazing power had been handed to me, an intuitive power that seemed to answer all my questions. It is as if I had been given my own private Guardian Angel, always at my side, always there to guide me. Of course there are times when I still feel confused or scared or angry. The difference is now that if I just take a moment to talk with my Teacher, the answers are there. Therefore the problems which before seemed to plague me now can be tremendous tools for growth."

A different answer to the question "what is my purpose in life" came when a person was not grounded enough in the physical world, and spent most of his or her time inwardly. The Teacher would nudge the person towards careers or goals. In that instance the answer sounded more like, "My wish for you is to return to school and learn a profession that allows you to develop your talents in working with people. It is there that you will find your purpose."

I recall reading for a lovely woman who, after one session, felt deeply connected to her Teacher. She told me that she connected to him every day and always followed his advice. She also complained, however, that the answers she received from her Teacher were not detailed and specific enough. I agreed to read for her again and see if there was anything we could do to help her get what she needed.

It wasn't very far into the reading when I realized that this woman wanted her Teacher to take total responsibility for her. She wanted her Teacher to be a good parent and tell her exactly what to do, step by step, and to make sure she never made a mistake, was never hurt, and never failed. The more this bright, dedicated woman demanded this from her Teacher, the less instruction she got. The session was growing more and more quiet and I thought the Teacher might disappear altogether when suddenly the Teacher's face was brighter than ever and his voice even more direct and clear. "Daughter, I cannot help you to steer your sailing ship until *you* create the wind," he said in a most loving and understanding voice. As he expanded this concept of personal responsibility, the woman was gratefully renewed in this awareness and as he continued to talk, I learned more about what makes a Teacher a true Master.

So often people wait for something outside of themselves, like a Teacher or spouse or child to create within them movement, desire or will. They say, "When you make me feel I can, I will. When you get me started, I will take over. When you show me how, I will do it." A Master Teacher will never agree to this bargaining. You must create your own will and make your own choices. Your Teacher will assist you even if you make a bad choice for yourself. They will not correct your mistake but will guide you into learning from it. They will answer your questions without robbing you of your journey. Rather than telling you exactly what to do, they will always help you to see truth.

I have been deeply moved by every Teacher I have met and in every reading was excited for the new things I learned. The most important part of each reading however, was finding out from each person's Teacher what they have to do to have direct access to their Teacher. Always the Teacher gave detailed instructions for the person based upon what that person is sensitive to and what will work for them. The instructions were as varied as the people but with some common structure. With a little practice people begin to hear and connect to their Teachers almost immediately, and I am grateful to have had a small part in their life-changing experience.

The Teachers are magnificent role models, and I could hardly believe my own enthusiasm for the readings, and for my unusual ability.

Part Three

MAKING CONTACT

How to Meet Your Master Teacher

The Teachers usually gave detailed and individualized instructions for contacting them during a reading, although there are some common techniques for everyone. In this chapter I will outline how to begin establishing direct contact with your Teacher and power animals. Please experiment and vary what you do until you find what works best for you. Your Teacher knows that you desire contact and will be there to assist you.

The first thing to remember is that what you put in your body will affect your pineal gland's ability to raise your frequency. While alcohol, caffeine, tobacco, recreational drugs and sugar will block your ability, other foods such as whole foods, organic fruits and vegetables, lemon and herbal teas may enhance your ability.

Be reassured that there is no danger at all in attempting to contact your Teacher. Your animals and Teacher are with you and would offer any protection if it were necessary. When your desire is to learn about what is in your highest good, You will not contact any "unfriendly" entities. In the hundreds of readings I've done, I never encountered any such thing.

The most common instruction I hear from a Teacher is: don't meditate. Meditation seems to lower our frequency which is very good for the body, for stress management, and for other spiritual practices but we are attempting to raise our frequency. The frequency of *imagination* is a higher frequency than that of *concentration*.

Do you remember when you were in school and started to feel bored? When you looked out the window you probably drifted into a deep and powerful daydream. That state of unfocused and unguided imagination is a very high frequency, high enough to interact with your Teacher. As you raise your frequency, your Teacher will lower his or hers, and you will establish contact. The most difficulty people seem to have is in believing it is too difficult. Contacting your Teacher is very easy, flowing and as natural as breathing. There are many times throughout the day when your frequency is naturally high, and you receive messages without realizing it. Due to this, you may sense a familiarity when you consciously make contact.

Vivian experienced that sense of familiarity:

"I think I have always been somewhat aware of my Teacher throughout my life, of her sweet gentle voice silently guiding me and comforting me throughout my joys and sorrows. Unfortunately I have not realized that sweet voice was indeed my Teacher's and so I have often ignored it. Yet as I look back through the years, I can see that even within my own cloud of distrust, I have somewhere always sensed her."

When our frequency is naturally high, we are more creative and intuitive and see things more clearly. At those times when we feel really "on," things seem to come to us more easily and with greater speed. All of us can recall times when we have felt this way naturally. Now, we want to reproduce that high frequency at will.

The setting needed will be different for everyone. Some will do well with little or no preparation and others will have more success utilizing a little ritual. Ritual can be lighting a candle, burning some incense, or playing some music, chanting, or drumming. Whatever you feel most comfortable with is fine.

First, try to establish contact with your eyes open as closing them can often lower your frequency. Allow yourself to drift into any fantasy or daydream you like while keeping your search for your animals and Teacher in mind. Do not force or guide the images or concentrate too hard. Many people find it easier to talk to their Teacher in the shower, or while walking or doing a mundane task since we tend to daydream at those times anyway.

At first your Teacher's "voice" will sound like your own thoughts inside your head. Trust this. As you practice you will eventually hear your Teacher's real voice inside your head and if you can get your frequency high enough, you may see your Teacher with your "third eye."

Barbara describes her experience this way:

"I must say that in just one session with you many questions were answered. For many years, there was a voice inside of me that I really never paid much attention to until our meeting. I realize that everyone has many sides to their personalities but there was always a different voice, one that was not under my control and seemed separate to me than the many facets of my personality. This voice influenced my beliefs and actions, but I always thought it was only my conscience speaking."

As you practice this, try sensing an energy or presence around you. This may feel like a warmth or tingling and is the energy of your Master Teacher or animal. There are subtle differences between us and our Teachers. Learning to distinguish the differences is vital to your faith in your Teacher and in your ability. As people incarnate, our awarenesses have a flat, logical, left-brain quality. The information is neither warm nor cold, hard nor soft. Our knowledge has a definite origin and end. Your Teacher's communication is different. Whether the information comes to you in words, thoughts, ideas, or pictures, the quality is subtly and distinctly different. Your Teacher's information will generally feel as though it has no origin, you suddenly "just know." The feeling is warm and softly flowing and settles not in the head, but in your whole body. Contact with your Teacher will produce an unmistakable, generalized feeling of love flowing in you and around you. The feeling of love seems to have no origin, source, or object. It is simply there and profoundly felt.

Information from your Teacher is also laced with feelings of love and colored with compassion, no matter what the topic. There may be a is a sense of oneness with all things. These qualities may feel different than what we generally experience regarding physical and body sensations. Remember that we are creatures who learn through our senses. All of our knowledge comes from what we can see, hear, smell, touch, and taste. Faith comes from what we learn *beyond* our senses, what we learn in spirit. Spirit is where you will connect with your Teacher most strongly, for that is their world. We cannot expect our Teacher to enter our corporal realm because they are spirit. We then must surrender our senses to our sixth sense: spirit.

Try to sense if your Teacher is male or female. Ask if there is a name they like to use. Use the first name that comes into your head. Continue asking questions and "sensing" answers. I use the word sensing because information comes in words only part of the time. The other times it will come in pictures, feelings, or warm sensations. Try to sense the energy presence of your Teacher in the room or near you. The lighter and more animated you keep your focus the easier the contact will be. In about two weeks of daily practice you will begin to develop a surer sense of your Teacher. Do not worry about whether or not you are "making up" the information. Your Teacher knows you are practicing and will find a way to covey the information to you even if it is through your own thought process. I have talked to my Teacher so often that I no longer need to day-dream for any contact. I just think of raising my fre-quency and I do. It is almost spontaneous, and this will happen for you too with practice.

If you find you are having difficulty, try new things. Burn a white candle or some incense. Try centering yourself first with prayer. Talk to your Teacher during different activities, or while taking a bath since water is very conductive. The possibilities are endless. The only caution I have is to not attempt this while driving. Sometimes the Teachers are quite compelling, and I wouldn't want you to be distracted from your driving.

There are some common positive signs of contact with your Teacher. These happen for some and not for others. When you have established contact, you may feel a tingling or warmth in your body. Some people report a little shiver occurs. You may feel an unmistakable feeling of love that seems to come from nowhere. You may suddenly be overcome with intense clarity. Everyone's reaction is a little differ-ent and if you are aware you will begin to notice yours.

Debbie reacted with resistance at first, as she tells here:

"At first, I had some resistance to talking to my Teacher, but as I continued I became less resistant. I wasn't always ready to listen to what my Teacher would communicate to me, but I trusted him and the process. I think mainly because he has always led me in a good direction. My life has undergone many changes since I've started to communicate with my Teacher and I've grown and gotten to know and love myself more and more from this process.

"What a beautiful feeling it is to know that someone is always there for me to call on for clarity and that I have this infinite source of love and wisdom at my fingertips. I can't imagine being without it."

Elaine had a completely different experience:

"Simply knowing I am not alone has been comforting and valuable. It's funny, too, because it is sort of like the chicken or the egg question. Are you the way you are and just happen to get along with your Master Teacher, or are you the way you are in good measure because of your Master

Teacher? I know Richard's (her Master Teacher) sense of humor—he can be very bawdy and outrageous at times! When I want to cheat on an eating plan or eat out of anger or frustration, I can almost audibly hear him say, "You're more than this. What is it you are really wanting?" I've yelled at him and told him and told him I was too tired, and I don't want to do this f--ing work anymore; we meet in meditations and walk together. In fact, before I met with you, that's when I first saw Richard. I'd arrive at a beautiful estate type residence, with pillars and a fountain in the center of the bottom floor and Richard was waiting for me. He was wearing a long gray monk's robe, tied at the waist. I asked if we could walk and said that I wanted to talk. I didn't have a clue who he was, I just knew he was a confidant or friend/advisor. It was like going home—here was my friend. He is ALWAYS there for me. When I get into a tailspin, I'm reminded of how I used to treat my son. Of course, there is no reaching someone who is having a tantrum, so I would just hold Ted gently until he was finished, then I would talk to him. Now Richard does the same with me."

Contact with your Teacher can occur easily with a little creativity and imagination. Thirteen year old

Crystal was speaking to Margaret one day when she asked her how to contact her Teacher. Margaret has great contact with her Teacher so she suggested to Crystal that she try to imagine what her Teacher might be like. Following Margaret's suggestion Crystal used writing as a creative outlet to help her connect to her Teacher. This is her story:

"It was a cold winter day in February. Elizabeth was sitting in the old oak tree reading her book in the backyard. While she was reading, she saw something out of the corner of her eye. She looked over to her left. Nothing was there. She looked all around her, but didn't notice anything different or out of place.

She looked up, her last possibility. She was surrounded with a bright, yet soft light. She heard a familiar voice. It was the sweetest voice she ever heard. The voice sounded strangely familiar; however, she could not figure out who it belonged to, or what it was trying to say.

After a confusing moment, she saw a face appear in front of her, about four feet away. Then soon after that she could see a full figure. This figure appeared to be singing. Even though Elizabeth couldn't tell what words it was singing, it was the most beautiful song she had ever heard.

Elizabeth watched it as it moved in circles around her. After it finished the song, it stopped in front of Elizabeth and just stared at her.

It was wearing a long, flowing, white, gown. She appeared to be some kind of angel. "Who are you?" Elizabeth said. She didn't answer "What is your name?" "Sarah," she said. "Where did you come from?" The being pointed to the clouds without taking her eyes off of Elizabeth. "Why are you here?" Again, Sarah didn't answer. Elizabeth said it again thinking that Sarah hadn't heard her in the first place. "For you." "What do you mean?" Sarah just looked at her. "Wha." "Be patient." "Be patient about what?" "Life. Be hopeful and you won't feel hopeless. Reach out to others for what you need, don't just put a wall around yourself. Be loving, and you will be loved. Trust, and you will be trusted. Understand, and people you know will listen." The figure faded back to a face. It's last words were, "Believe in yourself because I believe in you." And with that she disappeared completely, taking the light with her.

Elizabeth woke up in a cold, dark room. She was in her room laying on her back in the bed with the windows open. She was very confused. It was all a dream, and yet it seemed so real.

The next morning before school, Elizabeth went out to the old tree. She thought about what had happened in her dream. She found her book laying face-down on the ground with the pages shuffling in the wind. That's funny . . . she remembered taking her book in last night before she went to bed and put it on the nightstand. Next to the book she saw a soft glow. She reached out to touch it. It felt like silk. She picked it up. It was some kind of white dress that had probably torn when her mother was hanging the laundry. Or, could it be a long, flowing gown that belongs to an angel? She put it in her pocket and started walking to school.

When she got to class before the bell rang, Elizabeth walked over to the counter by the window to sharpen her pencil. As she reached into her pocket to get the pencil, the piece of cloth flew out of the open window and up towards the clouds. Elizabeth watched it as it glistened in the sun. She watched it until it slipped over the clouds in the blue sky. Then she heard Sarah's sweet voice calling her and saying, "I believe in you, and I'll always be here for you when you need me."

Elizabeth finished sharpening her pencil and went to her seat as her classmates were beginning to arrive . . .

Maybe it wasn't a dream after all."

I was very touched by Crystal's story, and I offered to read for her. I was curious about her process. Had she seen her Teacher or another guide? Was this her imagination? What was her power animal? Within weeks my questions were answered.

Meeting Crystal was not what I expected. Although she was thirteen, her soul and manner seemed somehow older and wiser. She was demure, mature, and openly loving. I asked her if the story was something from her imagination or something she had seen and experienced. She told me that she had actually seen the woman (Sarah) but wasn't sure who it was. I began the session with the usual auric cleansing. Her energy fields flowed well, and she had few blocks. I saw immediately that an eagle was sitting just to the left of her as she sat across from me. I told her that her power animal was an eagle. She smiled, blushed, and looked at the floor. "I thought it might be. I have been in love with eagles since I was a little girl!," she said softly. I shared with her the lesson of the eagle as being an animal that teaches the connection to the Divine and helped her to learn to communicate with the eagle that she would later name. As we spoke, the figure of her Teacher appeared on the other side of her. She excitedly spoke, "Hello! I am Sarah and I am Crystal's Teacher!" I was a little stunned, to say the least.

Crystal's reading flowed with no effort on my part. She was a very open person and as a result, she was easy to read for. I felt happy for her that at her youthful age she had managed to connect to her Teacher spontaneously, and openly. Her Teacher gave Crystal specific instructions for deepening their connection. She also assisted her with issues with her parents, relationships at school, and new ways to explore her creativity. Looking back on the experience I can see the lesson for me was that the *intention* to connect is, by far, the most important step in establishing a relationship with your Teacher.

Once you have established a connection with your Teacher your ability will continue to grow with practice. Your Teacher will become an integral and natural part of your life. My best friend Margaret shares her continued relationship with her Teacher:

"It was after Erika introduced me to my Teacher that I knew who I had been seeing and hearing for many years. I had been painting her for years in my artwork before learning that she was my Master Teacher.

"My first reading with Erika helped me to trust my intuition and experience and gave me a great sense of comfort to know she is always with me. My Teacher has a lightness of being and a sense of joy about her. She is passionate and intense in her being and communications with me. She is tender and warm, yet challenges me to face my fears and false beliefs and to move into my most loving state.

"I communicate with her in numerous ways. My favorite way is during my morning walk. I find that I can see and hear her more easily when I am moving and in nature. I start my walk each day with prayer and gratitude, then I move into dialogue with my inner child and then with my Teacher. I can see her in my inner vision and I hear her clearly. I can feel her presence around me. I also hear her constantly when I am working with clients. I can hear my client's Teacher as well. It is a great comfort to know that I have such profound assistance in my work with people.

"In the last two years two years my ability to see, feel and hear her has increased enormously and so has my faith. As a result my level of fear is almost non-existent much of the time. I am much more in the moment and able to maintain my sense of peace. I remember to live God's love. My mind-chatter is quelled. I know that I am not alone. There is a wealth of information available to me through my Teacher. As an author I have found that my writing process has changed. It used to take great effort to write now it is pure joy as I open to my Teacher and allow her to write through me. The same is true with public speaking which used to be frightening; it is now a joy. My connection to my Teacher has opened my path to God."

Your Teacher is a loving, devoted and compelling source of growth and knowledge. It is my wish that your relationship with your Teacher will be as gratifying and life-changing for you, as mine has been with my Teacher.

Part Four

THE TEACHINGS

I have kept a journal of my readings. In it I write down information the Teachers have conveyed to me, things I find particularly useful or wise or touching. In this section I will share that information with no particular order or story. For clarity I have used italics for my own words and explanations, and plain text for the words from the Teachers.

On Healing

"Color can heal. For example, inflammation is red and its opposite color, green can mute the inflammation, such as in vegetables. All disorders in the body have a specific color."

"Since foods have frequency like everything else, a person will find foods that are harmonic to him and foods that create dissonance. Some foods raise your frequency and some lower it. Sugar, alcohol and tobacco definitely interfere with the pineal gland's ability to raise frequency." *I have found that food plays an important role in my ability to see the Teachers. When I know that I will be reading for someone I*

take particular care to eat cleanly. Foods that contain sugar or preservatives cause me to struggle to raise my frequency. As a result the Teachers can appear wavy and unclear.

"Negative ion generators clear away negative energy as well. They are useful in therapy offices, etc. The generator, because of its frequency, will make contact with a Teacher very difficult and causes much static so it is best not to use one in the room when trying to contact a Teacher."

"Green candles create healing and peace for the body and soul. White candles bring in the Light while red candles honor your Teacher and those loved ones on the other side."

"Muscle testing (*kineseology)* is useful for testing food allergies, dissonant frequencies of objects and as a guide to taking supplements. To do this, hold the object being tested near your solar plexus since it is nearest the surface and most sensitive. Does the object make you feel anxious, tense, electrical or uncomfortable? If it does the object is dissonant to your frequency and not good for you. If the object makes you feel soft, relaxed and calm it is harmonic to your frequency and good for you." *This is an excellent way to test foods for you. Harmonic foods feel great and foods that are dissonant to your frequency will feel bad in your solar plexus.*

"Some people are color sensitive, and some are not. Some colors impact a person's frequency in a positive, harmonic way, like an overtone, while some colors are antagonistic and dissonant. The same is true of fabrics, metals, and materials; they all have a specific frequency. The idea that chakras can be healed by a specific color such as red for the base or purple for the third eye is erroneous. Red may be dissonant to the person in general and therefore does more harm than good. All of this is true for pitch and sound as well. Every individual resonates at a different frequency." *Have you noticed that some sounds and colors feel good to you and others make you feel uncomfortable? Try being more aware of how sounds and colors make you feel.*

"When doing memory exploration as part of any therapy, it is necessary to protect yourself from the psychic energy of past events. Although the re-experience of such events is sometimes necessary for healing, the psychic umbilical connecting you to people in the past is not healing and may be an obstruction to the healing process. To protect yourself and allow yourself a sense of safety, place your left arm across your heart and your right arm on top of the left whenever recalling past memories." *I had always noticed in my family therapy practice that when people would recall painful past events, they sometimes had difficulty letting go of the pain even after much of the material had been dealt with. I have experimented with this procedure and have observed that people are able to recall the past more easily, experience the pain, process the information without having a lingering effect. It seems that crossing your arm as the Teacher instructed breaks any psychic umbilical between the past and the present. In doing so, the present heals more quickly.*

"Stress is purely of the physical plane and need not be managed but discarded. You may guide your life with the energy of a fly, buzzing here and there with no real purpose but a lot of energy, or you can choose the energy of the butterfly, the symbol of transformation."

"Some conditions of the body are not put there to be cured but are there as a reminder to be humble enough to ask for help, and gracious enough to receive."

"Almond oil has a very high frequency and is very deflective. Used on the chakras, especially the solar plexus, it can help protect you from absorbing another's negative energy." *I have found this useful in sessions. It seems to protect me from taking in more energy that I should. It is also helpful after the breakup of a relationship, after arguments, or during stressful interactions.*

"What wounds you bring from childhood can be healed. Healing does not mean praying for the Light or asking the Light to come to you and thereby heal your wounds. Healing takes place only by remembering that you *are* the Light. The concept of needing the Light to come to you indicates that you believe that you are sitting in the darkness. The truth that heals is in knowing you are the Light." *I believe that all the therapeutic modalities that exist cannot heal in the way that this statement can. The idea that we are in fact Light addresses the issues of worth, love, value, personal responsibility, victimization, and self-worth— the very issues that cause us so much pain. People who believe that they are the way they are because of their childhood, rather than because of their* current *choices, are locked inside a prison of erroneous beliefs. Remembering your oneness with God and following that role model heals more than anything.*

On Children

"Even in adults, child-like play is important because it creates a state of daydreaming or imagination. Imagination is a very high frequency state naturally and so it is at those times you are most open to your Teacher." *Children seem to have more access to their Teachers and with more ease than adults. I have often thought that the state of wonder is actually a state of grace.*

"Children often fight with each other, especially siblings. The act of fighting is actually learning to handle and resolve conflicts. Parents tend to stop this behavior too soon, although they should be watchful for violence and anxiety. Remember that a flower that is hovered over and tended too much does not bloom well."

On Spirituality, Death, and Beyond

"All religions of the world are accurate and appropriate because they all lead eventually to the same Light. The difference between religions is the path the people need to travel to that Light."

"People constantly confuse preference with truth when they are indeed different. For example, your preference to believe in a certain concept does not ordain it as truth—it is simply preference. Truth is a virtue and of the spiritual level while preference is an earthly comfort. It is important to remember this when you have difficulty in accepting others'

religions, cultures, and values. *Arrogance transforms preference into an inflicted value.*

"Death is a transition to home. The planet is where we visit to grow and learn but most of our time is spent on the other side. A person transitions into the same level of awareness as he or she had on earth. Death does not bring instant enlightenment, but a new level and system of learning."

"Enlightenment means becoming part of the pure Light, part of the whole. God is the energy of the Light and each soul contains a piece of that Light. The Teachers have not yet reached enlightenment but are continuing their path towards it by working with you."

"Linear time and money are difficult concepts for the Teachers. Not only do they not exist in our world, but many of the Teachers existed on the planet before such things mattered. That is part of the reason fortune-telling type questions are difficult."

"The concept of gender is an earthly concept. Gender does not exist here. We are all equal souls."

"It is spirituality, not religion, that connects one to God. Religion is a passive connection while spirituality is active and interactive."

"One never has to worry about the outcome of things—it is your Teacher's job to manage the outcome. Faith is in knowing that the outcome will always be for your highest good, even if you don't get the outcome you want. Disappointment is only a sign that you cannot see the best outcome for yourself. You must trust that what isn't apparent will become apparent if you'll only wait. Looking to the past is a source of pain and frustration, while looking to the future helps you to create the movement in your life that your Teacher can assist with, so in order to have happiness, you must create it in the present and trust the outcome your Teacher has charge of." *Many people find this concept clear, yet*

difficult to do. A lot of us have strong control needs and feel anxious when we don't know the outcome or have control over it. So many times in my life I thought I knew what the outcome of something should be in order to support my growth. I would become invested in that outcome and angry if it didn't happen the way I thought it should. Usually, months later, I would hear myself thinking "God, I'm glad it didn't work the way I wanted it. It would have been a mess!" Now as I let go more and more and trust my Teacher with the outcome, I feel more at peace and less frantic. I know that in everything, there is a purpose.

"Ask yourself each day if what you are doing is serving the Universe (God) or is self-serving. Anything that is self-serving is a waste of spirit. Learning to love yourself and through devotion to loving others is serving God." *This concept naturally raises questions about devotion to others and co-dependent caretaking. When I asked my Teacher about this, she explained to me that co-dependence is earthly and part of the struggle of earthly love whereas devotion to others is a spiritual concept. You cannot be devoted to the service of others and God if you are not spiritu-*

ally grounded enough to love yourself by taking care of yourself. Sometimes, this means setting limits.

"Most people in their desire to have healthy relationships have forgotten the concept of devotion to others. It is only through devotion to others that you can truly grow spiritually and come closer to God. In this realm, caretaking does not exist, we all serve each other and thereby, God."

"Archangel is the closest English concept to the Master Teachers. However, an archangel is passive while a Master Teacher is active and interactive. Jesus was the greatest Master Teacher of all and we commonly consult with Him and seek out His advice."

"Holy Spirit is the intention to connect to a higher source, not an entity."

"It is a Universal Law that just as the rivers are compelled to flow towards the ocean, so it is that the Light is compelled to flow towards the darkness. Sometimes there are storms at sea, and in that storm the sea will flow back into the river almost as though it were lashing out at the river. So too, can darkness lash out at the Light in times of crisis. In these times the Light is compelled to help the darkness. This is especially important to remember in relationships. A healthy, earthly marriage means that two people are dedicated to each other's happiness and growth. However, the person in the Light may be compelled to flow towards the person who is in the dark. It is important to remember that our primary relationship is with God and our secondary relationship is with another person." *This concept took me awhile to understand and I will try to clarify it more. When I saw couples in therapy I very often saw that the relationship had become askewed. That is, one person is in a needy, confused role and the other seems to be more stable. In an effort to stabilize their relationship the couple will enter into a co-dependent relationship with one care-taking the other and trying to make him or her okay. The Light flows towards the darkness. The person who is having the difficulty, while wanting the help, will often feel more helpless due to their partner's care-taking. Very often, that helplessness will result in the person feeling angry and lashing out at the one who is offering the caretaking. The darkness lashes out at the Light. The important awareness is that this relationship is secondary to the individual relationships each has with God. Most people forget this and spend their time trying to "fix" the relationship rather than grow spiritually and individually.*

"A prayer without love cannot be answered." *This statement was in response to my asking about the power of prayer. It means that a prayer that is pleading in nature, rather than one that results when feeling connected to God, misses the connection altogether. Without establishing love first, there is only a one-way connection. Hence, the answer cannot be returned.*

"There is no reward in suffering. "

"You cannot manipulate or teach another to face their unlovingness. You have to love them into their self-awareness." *This means that trying to get another*

to change doesn't work and isn't loving. By becoming more loving ourselves we create an environment in which a person may feel safe enough to look into the mirror. There are no guarantees, and they may never look, but in any case we have moved ourselves into a higher level of growth. To become more loving in order to get someone to change is the highest form of manipulation.

"Everything you do, think, and feel affects your soul."

"One cannot become a spiritual leader until they have surrendered their will to God's. Understanding God's will for you is the primary purpose of growth."

On Divine Love

"Think of Divine Love as a two-sided coin. On one side of the coin is the doctrine: Never walk by another who is in pain without tending to their wound. On the other side of the coin is the doctrine: Never allow another to sacrifice for you. It is each person's responsibility to live both doctrines. Some will find however, that they naturally do one with ease while struggling with the other. That is the nature of growth, to find balance, and to become both." *The Teacher did not imply that you tend to another's wound by taking responsibility for their wound or their healing. Sometimes, the only way you can attend to another's wound is by surrounding them with love and light. If another person is giving to you and it makes them happy it is not a sacrifice. Learning to let love in is just as important as learning to be loving.*

"If another gives to you with joy, accept their gift with gladness. If however, another gives to you with duty, expectations or responsibility, set them free."

"Guilt is the nagging feeling that you have let yourself down."

"If you see another in emotional pain and though that pain be expressed as anger, tend to their wound. In doing so, you heal your own." *Again that does not mean you have to take responsibility for their pain but maybe you can send them love. On the other hand, we are not so fragile that we can't sometimes deflect the anger expressed at us and steadfastly love the person. Parents do this with angry toddlers all the time. They don't feel hurt by the child—they just feel love. Is this allowing yourself to be abused? The answer depends on your intention. Words thrown in anger have no potential to wound us unless we give that person the power to define who we are. If we*

know we are God, we can't be hurt by their words. Physical abuse is a different matter—never let anyone physically hurt you.

"There are three levels to your being—the earthly, physical level, the emotional level and the spiritual level. Although you can't help but be drawn to the physical and emotional because you live there, you must aspire to live in the spiritual level." *I asked for further clarification of these levels and was able to understand it more fully. The physical and emotional levels are inherent in being in a body. On these levels we tend to see our being as existing in this lifetime only. We are concerned with our happiness, relationships, work, family, and health. We relate to each other in those terms and think of our growth as having a result this lifetime. These levels are very outward directed. On the spiritual level we know we are one with God as well as God's representative here on the planet. We are concerned with loving others and mankind as well as healing our planet. We know our growth extends beyond the limits of our bodies into a time continuum and our relationships are but miniature classrooms in which to learn to love as God. The*

spiritual level is more inward. During any moment we exist in one of these three levels. Every interaction, action and feeling can be defined as one of these levels. Our job is to try and exist on the spiritual level as much as possible. We can do this at work, in our relationships and within ourselves. That is what our Teachers assist us with.

"What you call love, we here on this side refer to as earthly love rather than Divine Love. For you, love is a rhythm of a breath out and a breath in. It is giving and receiving. For us, our breath out is our breath in. To this you can aspire and grow spiritually. Words like codependence and caretaking describe earthly love and have no meaning in Divine Love, because earthly love encompasses only one lifetime rather than a continuum. Earthly love expects something. Divine Love loves for its own sake. Each person has the choice to love on an earthly level or with Divine love."

"You have long believed that it is better to teach a hungry man how to fish rather than to give him a fish to eat and that is true. Yet, one cannot be so arrogant as to decide when a person should be full enough to fish for himself. It may take many, many fish for a person to feel full enough to learn and sometimes that may mean more than one lifetime. So it is with love that a person may require much love before they are strong enough to be loving. In earthly love you expect to see change and growth in that person immediately and in this lifetime as a result of your loving them. In Divine Love, no results are ever expected—the person will heal when they heal. Now, or in the hereafter, or perhaps the next lifetime."

∾

"God gave people the capacity to know what they want and very often people are motivated by what they want and this is fine. But with the freedom to want, comes the responsibility for the actions and consequences to others that getting what you want may have. For example, you may want to do something special, and you think to some degree about the impact it has on others. Most people do not look around a full three-hundred-sixty degrees to see how their choices affect others. In fact, when it comes to wanting, most people have tunnel vision—a kind of selective vision that cannot see any hurt they can cause by fulfilling their want. Remember to make an intelligent, informed decision *prior* to taking action. Having the means to get what you want doesn't mean that it is a good choice. Sometimes getting what you want on an earthly level negates getting what you want on the spiritual level: being a being of Divine Love."

"Sacrifice on an earthly level means doing something you don't really want to do for another. On the level of Divine Love, the word does not exist. All giving is joy."

I once asked my Teacher about the concept of boundaries and limit setting with regards to relationships. I wanted to know how to set boundaries in a loving way. Her answer was very thoughtful: "There are no boundaries on our side because they aren't needed. We do not violate each other here. I know you believe that people, in general, have difficulty setting limits. It would be more helpful for you to explore the difficulty people have in accepting the limits and bound-aries placed on them by others. That is the more difficult task. The pursuit of establishing boundaries in a loving way so as to make them more acceptable to the other person is a waste of spirit."

"As Mother Teresa has said," I am just God's pencil" and that is what acceptance truly is. Acceptance is a fine thing, for in its center, one finds spiritual peace. Yet one day, God may throw his pencil into the center of darkness and at that moment, the pencil, through its devotion to God, becomes The Word."

"As with all students, students of spirituality are given tests. The test will come as an argument, accusation, failure, disappointment or perhaps something you cannot control. It is your chance to show what you have learned; not what you understand or what you believe, but who you are ready to become. There are no grades or judgments with this test, it is just an expression of your devotion to God. Who you are willing to become, is how you love God."

"Divine Love is God, and within you is the capacity to love Divinely."

On Faith

"Faith is not supported by the senses. If anything, trusting your physical senses about God takes you far from home."

"It is not enough to seek out and develop a personal relationship with God. You must be God's warrior and not accept darkness when you see it."

"When you substitute what you can perceive with your senses for your faith, you destroy your faith."

One day I was sitting alone and pouting about an argument I had just had. I felt frustrated and justified in my anger and suddenly my Teacher came to me with this insight. "All of you experience anger from the same belief, the belief that you are not being seen by someone. Being seen is very important to you because it validates you. What you always forget is that the only one who can always see you is God. To have this expectation of consistent sight from someone you love is an unreasonable demand. Your feelings of safety do not depend upon another person, but upon God. Rest your fears and worry with Him, He wants the job." *Her voice was filled with so much compassion and love that I immediately felt calm again. I have since carried the thoughts with me and if I start to feel angry with someone I am able to acknowledge the feeling, know that I am seen, and continue on, leaving my anger behind.*

"Shame is the feeling of guilt turned-inside-out."

"God is not capable of creating anything imperfect, that is why you were created with the ability to love. The heart is the symbol of pure perfection."

"Faith is never born of crisis. Faith is something you must accumulate every single day so that, should the need arise, you will have more than enough to cover any challenge."

"To acquiesce is to concede in despair. To surrender is to become One with God."

"When the fingers of your knowledge are stretched to their limit, they touch unto faith. Hope is born in the marriage of faith and knowledge."

"You came from a state of Grace and there again you shall return. Everything in between is but a thrill-ride of learning."

"As you love a puppy with delight, understanding, and protection, so does God love you especially when you are at your worst."

"When you relax, you open the door to active prayer. Active prayer allows you to move into contemplative prayer and from there you move into a state of Grace."

"Inspiration is when you reach out and take God's hand into yours."

"To give up is to be alone and passive. Surrender is an active expression of faith in something higher."

"A person receives from God according to his ability to receive. That ability is determined by his level of faith."

"When your devotion to another becomes conditional, so is your devotion to God. How you relate to each other is the mirror of your soul's intent with God."

"All actions are the expressions of your faith, and faith the expression of your actions."

Questions

Early in my relationship with my Teacher, I had a need to ask many general questions. This was due, in part, to my own curiosity and also, I think I had some need to test this new source of information. I sat with my tablet, pen and list of questions and found her energy to be understanding and encouraging. She was patient with my questions as well as my skepticism. The following is a transcript of those sessions.

Teacher, tell me what God is . . . is God a "HE"?
"Before I answer the many questions I sense you have, I want you to understand that these answers are for you. Another person asking their Teacher the same questions would receive answers for them. You see, I can answer you according to your level

of understanding and your frame of reference. Now before you interpret this as a disclaimer, try to open your mind a little. I will speak to you of what you know—it is that simple. God is the hardest concept to describe. God is larger than you can understand being in a physical body and more complex than you can experience but see if you can feel what I say. God is the collective energy of love and of all that is. God is oneness, life, and love. Each of you contains within your soul a seed of this same greatness. In that sense you are one, and a co-creator with God. God is the sum of all that is good and gracious. The idea that God has gender is not quite accurate. Gender is of the body . . . where you are. There are no physical bodies in God's realm, so gender is not here. The concept of God as "He" is something that was created long ago by people. It was a necessary concept in its time, for being limited to language, there had to be a pronoun to use. The masculine pronoun implied a greater power at that time than the feminine."

Are you telling me that God is not a Supreme Being? I was taught this since I was little!

"I am telling you that God is **even more** than the concept of a being. God's greatness cannot be confined to a being, Supreme or otherwise. Even as you and I communicate now, we are limited to words and the pictures I can communicate to you. Still, it is not enough when we try to define God. I understand your need to visualize something when you think of God. Rather than a being, it is more accurate to visualize energy. Better still, try to **feel** God."

But there are many who believe in God as a Supreme Being, or others who believe that the Spirit of God is in all things like trees, rocks, or animals. Are they wrong?
"Of course not! They believe what they are comfortable with. There are many paths to God. God is love and if their beliefs lead them to love, they are on a good path."

What happens when we die?
"I can tell that question holds much fear for you. That is alright daughter, it is only natural to fear what you have not yet experienced. When your time comes, your soul will leave its body **before** you draw your last breath. The body ceases breathing because it is no longer occupied. There is no feeling of suffocation or gasping. It is more like walking into another room.

You are never alone in the process. Your loved ones and your Teacher come and hold your hand to support you in your transition."

How about the tunnel so many people describe when they die and are brought back?
"A tunnel is a good description. As the soul leaves the body it is like passing through a tunnel at high speed. The walls of the tunnel are actually matter as seen through eyes that are in transition."

Is the white light God?
"It is the first contact with God, although God is even greater."

Are we judged when we get there?
"There is no one who judges you. You will be offered a review of your own life and your choices. You will be the only judge. You will decide for yourself if you learned what you wanted to learn. In God's loving realm you are discouraged from berating yourself. There simply is what is."

When does the soul enter the body?

"Just as you would not move into a new home before it is finished, the soul enters the body when its home is complete . . . just before birth."

How about hell, does it exist?

"Transitioning does not mean you actually go anywhere, except for another dimension at first. Those who have left are still with you and around you at times. There is another life here that is more of an extension of your existence there. Generally, people who have recently transitioned like to stay near those they love. They watch and love and help. As the soul grows and evolves, they find new goals and work and move to continually higher levels. Heaven is a state of Grace where the soul is compelled towards knowledge and love. Hell is the opposite state. A state of darkness, unlovingness, and resentment. When a person transitions their experience is largely determined by their beliefs. If a soul has a deep expectation for punishment, they may find themselves in darkness. As soon as they even think of love and light they are again in the Lightness of God. Their Teacher is there to help but first the person must have a true desire to be helped. Those who believe in a loving God find what they expect. The choice is always up to the individual here as it is on earth. You can choose the darkness or the lightness, love or suffering."

You mean all I have to do is believe in God's lovingness and I will go to a state of Grace?
Almost. To truly believe in God's love you must be willing to honor God by always becoming more loving yourself."

I knew it was too easy.
"Oh, Daughter. I did not say you had to have perfect love. I said the intention to love was all that was required to transition into God's love. There are many levels, and you will one day see that it is not as black and white as you like to make things (laughing)."

Okay, so is there a devil lurking around trying to recruit souls for the darkness?
"Remember how I told you that God is more like an energy. . . . the collective energy of love? Well there is also a collective energy of darkness. This energy

feeds on fear and greed and unlovingness in general. You do not become a part of the darkness unless you choose to through your beliefs and your actions. Mistakes do not damn you to the darkness—being closed to becoming love does it. Are your thoughts more of love or something darker?"

I think more about being loving, even when I screw up. But I was raised with the belief that we all sin and we must all pay for those sins, and we can't help but be sin.

"Don't confuse sin with being human. The only true sin is in not being devoted to love God and to love others. Even then if you spend a time in your life angry, needy, and unloving, you still have the choice at any time to renew your devotion to God. Instead of sin try using the word unloving. It will make things easier for you. The Kingdom of God is love, and that Kingdom of God is within."

What about the Commandments then?

(smiling) "Daughter, the Commandments are there to help guide you to lovingness!"

Are men and women equal or were women created to serve men?

"People were put on earth to serve God by serving each other. The concept that women are subservient is not a Divine concept."

How about races? Why are there so many? Why weren't we all one race?

"God likes beauty. Would you want there to be only one kind of flower? The difficulties between races comes from a lack of acceptance for each other and for God's will."

Does God hear our prayers?

"Absolutely!! Especially those prayers that are prayed in a state of love. But aren't you really asking me if God **answers** your prayers?"

Uh, . . . okay. I guess that's true.

"In your thoughts I can hear you testing God's love for you almost daily. If you get what you want, it means God loves you. If you don't get what you want, your faith suffers. Would you like me to teach you to deepen your prayer?"

I feel unsure about your offer.

"I will always honor your wishes, Daughter. I will stand with you always in your prayer. Would you like to talk of something else?"

No thank you Teacher. Not right now. (Days passed while I wrestled with my hesitation. I finally realized that I was afraid of having the safety of my traditions and beliefs in prayer threatened.)

Teacher, tell me about prayer.

"I rejoice in your courage, Daughter. Each step brings you closer to God. First, it is important to recognized that all thought is energy. Prayer, when well done, is the movement of energy. The very first step is to **relax** and establish a feeling of love in your heart. Without love, you are not connected to God. Next, is active prayer. That is, you speak openly to God. This helps move you into contemplative prayer where God speaks to you. Too often, people spend their precious moments in prayer trying to elicit God's help so that the outcome of something will be **their** outcome. That is forsaking God's will for yours. It is far higher to pray for clarity and acceptance of God's will than to plead for a specific outcome. Remember that you are the extension of God's spirit. You are God's representative of love here on earth."

Thank you. That is very clarifying for me. I have very many questions for you. Some, I know the answers to and others I am not sure of.

"Where you need reassurance, you shall have it. Where you need truth, you shall have that, too. What do you want to know?"

Is the Bible the true word of God?

"The spirit of the Bible is to teach love and that **is** God's word. Remember though that the Bible has been translated and therefore, changed. Each word is not necessarily a direct quote. The spirit of the Bible is the spirit of God."

What about those who choose things like suicide?

"To throw away the gift of life is a very sad choice for all of us. When you leave the physical body, your soul continues in its entirety. That means that the problems that caused such distress in life of the suicide victim are still with the soul on the other side. It is always better to finish the life you are given. With suicide, there are Teachers here who work with that lost soul and help it to move closer to the Light. Suicide is a very large step away from God.

Sometimes it is necessary for this soul to sleep a long time before it is ready to heal."

What do you mean "sleep"?
"A soul that has darkened itself will often transition to a place of quiet where it remains dormant for some time. All the while a Teacher stands by, ready to help the moment the soul reaches for God. A darkened soul, what you might call evil, has great energy, confusion, and turmoil. The dormant period is for soothing rather than punishment, although a dark soul will sometimes create punishment as a way of atonement. Even that choice makes us very sad because it is not necessary. The dark soul could also choose love."

You have clearly implied that we do reincarnate. How does this work? Are we told when to come back? Do we have to?
"No one forces a soul to return to the body. Yet, we choose to do so because the body and the planet provide us some of the best challenges for our soul's growth. Those on this side regard you in the body as the heroes. It takes courage and devotion to return

to the body and you do so solely on a voluntary basis. You choose the time, the body and the life that will suit your needs to grow. The option to do this is truly a gift from God. There are some who choose to remain here for eons. That is their choice and is right for them. Here, as there, the path of growth is still up to the individual soul."

But it seems like we always forget why we came here. Why don't we just remember?
"Actually, a few do remember. Then there are those who get lost and don't remember their plan. Even that can be part of the plan. To find yourself in the darkness, yet demonstrate enough faith to go home in Light, is a far greater challenge and statement of devotion than to be born into the Light and retain it your entire life.

You said that God is love. In the realm of spirit what do you call love? It is different than how we define it?
"Yes, there is a great difference between earthly love and Divine love. You shall learn more of this in days to come and from other Teachers as well."

Love is a hard concept in any realm! I understand your meaning of God as love, but I still don't understand why there is so much suffering here. Especially for children who are abused or starving. Where is God's love for them?

"You ask a very heartfelt question. God promised free will to all people. If God were to lovingly end all suffering your free will would end, too. It is the responsibility of all people to end suffering. One of the reasons the planet makes such an excellent classroom is that there is a balance of Light and dark, of good and bad. The suffering you see is there for all souls to conquer through your own devotion and love. Even the smallest child is a volunteer, a hero. Children are born innocent and loving but not without a plan. When I have fulfilled my duties as a Master Teacher I may then choose to return to the body as a small child of a hungry nation. There I will use my spiritual power to live in the struggle, knowing I can and will prevail with God's love. This is my offer of love, to be used as a lesson and a point for those who wish to conquer darkness. A young soul in the early stages of growth would not be given such an incarnation. Those who ease the suffering and those who suffer each offer a unique gift. It is only through devotion and love and our oneness with God that the planet will be rid of suffering for all. This is our quest and our journey. Remember that human suffering is always the result of human fault."

I understand the role of the innocent but what about those who seem to take actual pleasure in harming others?

"You speak of the young souls with the fewest incarnations. They do take pleasure in the dark energy. For them to find God means that we must love them in spite of themselves. In a sense we share our Light with them until their own begins to awaken. Eventually, when they can at least see the love, they can begin to move towards it, towards God."

In truth I don't think I can walk up to someone who is harming another and say I love you.

"Maybe not. But you can surround them with prayer and the love of God in your thoughts and wishes. Imagine the soul who could be surrounded by many in the Light—enveloping them with Divine Love— that could not be moved! The love of many souls will always create the healing force of God. Think of the darkest soul that ever walked the planet."

I can think of a number of them throughout history.
"Good. Now imagine if God's people had all prayed for that one soul. Do you think that history would have been the same?"

No, that's hard to imagine.
"This then is the lesson of loving your enemies. In hatred and anger you join the darkness, in prayer and love you join God."

Teacher, how should I measure my spiritual growth?
"By the love for all things in your heart. As your love grows, so does your oneness with God. Remember that it is only through service to others that one can truly grow spiritually."

Service?
"Service can be expressed in every word, deed ,and thought. That does not mean your vocation. It means who you choose to be. In your family, in your psychology practice, in your daily tasks and in your recreation, there are endless opportunities to serve. Greater opportunities to serve happen as one grows

away from self and towards community. When you serve each other, you also serve God. Remember that all of your actions are an expression of your faith"

Thank you Teacher. I really love our talks. You help me to stretch and to grow. I really do feel your love. What can I do for you now?

"Remember that I am with you always Child, and in the coming days let us pray for each other."

I always will Teacher.

Epilogue

Since my work with the Teachers, it has been fascinating for me to note the changes in my life and in me. Prior to that first meeting with my Teacher, I was inebriated with the successes of my first two books and living a lifestyle that matched my growing notability.

On a personal level I was more in the fast lane of life playing with my yacht in Marina del Rey and driving the best luxury cars, flying every plane I could get my hands on. My work was growing at a hectic pace as my family therapy practice was thriving and I was doing more and more radio and television shows, lectures, and workshops. I was surrounded by people and seemed to be very happy living the American dream. I could not, at that time, conceive of anything better. The downside was, however, my impatience and judgmentalness. I was into instant gratification and righteousness. After all, I had become a sought-after expert and demanded the perks and quirks that I knew were due to me. I was aware of the flaws in my demanding behavior, yet even the "expert" in me felt confused about healing it. Besides, nobody was perfect, and I had so much to offer! My motivation to grow was interfering with all the fun I was having.

I laugh at me then from this vantage point in time. I notice that I prefer my Mickey Mouse watch to my expensive one, and I drive truck around Colorado, and thrive in my simple life on my horse ranch. I would rather spend my time training horses than anything else. I traded my love of flying for a fishing rod and a kayak. There is suddenly time enough for everything and being recognized is now more of an embarrassment. My work has been reborn. I no longer do family therapy or have a private practice, or do readings for people. I am content as an ordained Interfaith chaplain and at peace as "God's pencil."

I delight in promoting Inner Bonding with co-creator Dr. Margaret Paul, as I see the enormous impact and healing for people all around the world now.

The Six-Step Inner Bonding process is a direct result of our relationship with our Teachers.

My Teacher has brought me far. Sometimes I wonder at the marvel of God's design to gift us with such patient and devoted Teachers. I am saddened too sometimes at the thought of those who have no awareness of this process. My Teacher has taken me to God and in return I work to serve others now with the same devotion I have been shown.

Life is, for me, now soft and flowing. Not necessarily easy, but filled with love, hope, laughter, and faith. When life becomes heavy with challenges and obstacles, I have the faith and teaching to see me through. I am not alone. I am a little older now, and a little more caring now. I hope for you the closeness with God and your Teacher that I have come to love. I leave you with this gift from my Teacher and me.

My Teacher's Prayer

Oh, Loving Spirit and the Spirit of my Ancestors,
Help me to transcend my physical being.
Help me to hear the rocks that I may learn
    patience.
Help me to feel the trees that I may know persistence.
And help me to hear the four-leggeds that I may
    know wonder.

I pray for the ancient winds to blow gentle
    openness into my heart,
And for the Light Of Life to fill me with Your
    wisdom.

Let me see your vision that I may know my own,
And never let me forget your voices that I may hear
    my own calling.

Loving Spirit, teach me to pray that I may continue
your prayers.

Ancient Teachers,
Feel my offer of love that I may know my own
lovingness,
And in the completion of the sacred Circle,
Step into the Light and complete my mission as a
Master.

All this I pray,
That I may become forever
Peace and Divine Love.
Amen

www.ingramcontent.com/pod-product-compliance
Lightning Source LLC
Jackson TN
JSHW010244070325
80335JS00013B/791